Artists in Profile

SURREALISTS

Linda Bolton

Heinemann
LIBRARY

First published in Great Britain by Heinemann Library, Halley Court, Jordan Hill, Oxford OX2 8EJ, part of Harcourt Education. Heinemann is a registered trademark of Harcourt Education Ltd.

© Harcourt Education Ltd 2002
The moral right of the proprietor has been asserted.

Editorial: Jilly Attwood and Claire Throp
Design: Jo Hinton-Malivoire and Tinstar Design Limited (www.tinstar.co.uk)
Picture Research: Catherine Bevan
Production: Lorraine Warner

Originated by Ambassador Litho Ltd
Printed and bound in China by South China Printing Company

ISBN 0 431 11652 0
06 05 04 03 02
10 9 8 7 6 5 4 3 2 1

British Library Cataloguing in Publication Data
Bolton, Linda
   Surrealists. - (Artists in profile)
   709'.04063

A full catalogue record for this book is available from the British Library.

Acknowledgements
The publishers would like to thank the following for permission to reproduce photographs: AKG/Bianconero pp**11**, **15**, AKG/Tony Vaccaro p**20**; Artothek/Foundation P Delvaux-St Idesbald, Belgium/DACS, London 2002 p**19**, Artothek/ADAGP, Paris and DACS, London 2002 p**24**; Boston, Museum of Fine Arts/AKG/2002 Banco de Mexico Diego Rivera & Frida Kahlo Museums Trust. p**31**; Buffalo (N.Y.) Albright-Knox Art Gallery /AKG/ ADAGP, Paris and DACS, London 2002 p**45**; Camera Press p**18**; Cologne, Museum Ludwig/AKG/ADAGP, Paris and DACS, London 2002 p**4**; Corbis/Burstein Collection/DACS 2002 p**12**, Corbis/Burstein Collection/Succession Marcel Duchamp/ADAGP, Paris and DACS, London 2002 p**21**,Corbis/Paul Almasy p**27**, Corbis/Archivo Iconografico, S.A/ADAGP, Paris and DACS, London 2002 p**36**, Corbis/Marianne Haas p**39**, Corbis/Geoffrey Clements/Man Ray Trust/ADAGP, Paris and DACS, London 2002 p**48**; Hulton Archive p**35**; Kuntsmusum, Basel, Switzerland/ Bridgeman Giraudon/ Lauros/ADAGP, Paris and DACS, London 2002 p**28**; Landeau Collection, Paris/Bridgeman/Giraudon/Lauros/ADAGP, Paris and DACS, London 2002 p**23**; Lee Miller. Lee Miller Archives, Chiddingly, England p**52**; Minneapolis Institute of Arts, MN USA/Bridgeman Art Library/ ARS, NY and DACS, London 2002 p**51**;Museo Picasso, Barcelona/Bridgeman Giraudon/ Lauros/ADAGP,Paris and DACS, London 2002 p**43**; Museum of Fine Arts, Houston, Texas/Bridgeman Art Library/Louise Bourgeois/VAGA, New York/DACS, London 2002 p**54**; Museum of Modern Art, New York/SCALA / Salvador Dalí, Gala-Salvador Dalí Foundation, DACS, London 2002 p**17**; Private Collection/Bridgeman Art Library/2002 Banco de Mexico Diego Rivera & Frida Kahlo Museums Trust p**32**; Private Collection/Bridgeman Art Library/ADAGP, Paris and DACS, London 2002 pp**40**, **53**; Tate, London 2002/Salvador Dalí, Gala-Salvador Dalí Foundation, DACS, London 2002 p**8**; Telimage p**5**, Telimage/Man Ray Trust/ADAGP, Paris and DACS, London 2002 pp **7**, **47**, **50**.

The cover photograph shows *Son of Man* by René Magritte (1964). This image is reproduced with permission of Bridgeman/ADAGP, Paris and DACS, London 2002.

Our thanks to Richard Stemp for his help in the preparation of this book.

Author dedication
For my daughter Portia with love.

Contents

Words appearing in the text in bold, **like this**, are explained in the Glossary.

What is Surrealism?

Surrealism is one of the most important art movements of the 20th century. It transformed not only painting and sculpture, but also literature, theatre and the cinema and even the way people thought about their lives. The word 'surreal' has entered our language to describe anything that is weird, bizarre or dreamlike, not simply in art, but in life itself.

The Surrealists rejected the logical world of reason and tried to explore the unthinking, or **unconscious**, part of their minds. They were fascinated by dreams, and many of them painted weird, dreamlike visions. The Surrealists were also interested in the imagination of children and the insane, which they saw as being uncorrupted by reason.

In their attempt to explore the unconscious mind, some Surrealists developed a method of **automatic** writing and painting. Artists tried to approach their work without any thought beforehand, returning to a childlike state in order to produce works of pure imagination.

The Rendezvous, by Max Ernst (1922–23)
This work by Ernst shows many of the participating members of the Surrealist group, including de Chirico, Breton and Ernst himself.

The Surrealists were struck by the magical, the marvellous and the unexpected. They looked for beauty in unusual places and objects, and in everyday objects placed in unexpected settings. 'Beauty should seize you by the throat,' said Lautréamont, a 19th-century French poet who the Surrealists admired. He declared that beauty should be surprising like 'the chance encounter of a sewing machine and an umbrella on the operating table' and this dramatic image appealed strongly to the Surrealists' sense of the bizarre.

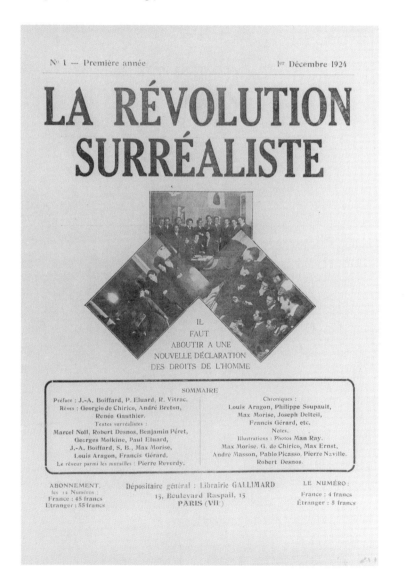

■ In 1924 André Breton founded the magazine La Révolution Surréaliste, which he edited, and which was the most important publication of the movement from 1924 to 1929.

Surrealism was practised across all the art forms – painting, sculpture, poetry, film, jewellery, dress and ceramic design. Dedicated Surrealists even lived their lives in a surreal way, performing consciously eccentric antics. These surreal gestures could be quite extreme, such as Salvador Dalí's lecture in a diving suit, but could also be much less obvious, like René Magritte's small but surprising rebellions in a life of apparent respectability.

André Breton and Surrealism

The Surrealist movement began officially in Paris in 1924, when the French poet, novelist and critic André Breton wrote his first *Surrealist Manifesto* – a document laying out the aims of the new movement. In this **manifesto** Breton defined Surrealism as a movement in which imagination rules. He wrote, 'Only imagination makes me aware of the possible.' Breton took the name 'Surrealist' from the poet Guillaume Apollinaire who described his play, *Les Mamelles de Tirésias* (The Breasts of Tiresias), performed in 1917, as a 'surrealist drama'.

For Breton, the dream was the most important thing in art and in life. He was very interested in the findings of the Austrian doctor Sigmund Freud, who had made a study of the **unconscious**, which he believed was largely revealed through dreams. Freud thought that by interpreting the meaning of his patients' dreams he could help them to recover from disturbing mental conditions. In 1921, Breton visited Freud in Vienna and returned to Paris even more interested in the unconscious, and especially in dreams. He gathered about him a group of poets and painters who were also fascinated by the world of dreams.

Sigmund Freud 1856–1939

The ideas and methods of the Austrian psychiatrist Sigmund Freud had a powerful influence on the Surrealists. Freud was very interested in the dreams that his patients described to him. He believed that dreams revealed people's secret wishes and fears, and in 1900 he published a massive study, *The Interpretation of Dreams*. Like Freud, the Surrealists explored the world of dreams. They also adopted Freud's method of **free association** – a way of discovering important events in his patients' lives by encouraging them to talk about whatever came into their heads. Surrealist artists and writers used free association to create their **automatic** art.

Breton encouraged Surrealist poets and writers to publish their work in his magazine, *La Révolution Surréaliste*, which he edited from 1924 to 1929, and in 1933, the glossy magazine of Surrealism called *Minotaur* was founded. As well as writing poems and creating works of art, the Surrealists also produced plays and films. These include Man Ray's *Emak Bakia* and Salvador Dalí and Luis Buñuel's *Un Chien Andalou*.

The first Surrealist exhibition was held in Paris in 1925, but the movement soon spread beyond France. The Surrealists came from a wide range of countries, with major artists working in France, Germany, Belgium, Switzerland, Spain and even Mexico and the USA.

Dada

Although Breton's manifesto of 1924 marked the official start of Surrealism, the movement actually had its roots in an earlier art movement known as **Dada**, which began in Switzerland in 1916. The Dadaists were powerfully affected by the horrors of World War I (1914–18). They believed that if reason and logic had led to the mass destruction and horror of war, then perhaps the opposite of reason and logic might provide a better alternative. Dada was an anti-art movement which wanted to destroy traditional methods of painting and sculpture and make something entirely new. The Dadaists created random images by dropping torn fragments of paper, by displaying **found objects** like bottle racks and bicycle wheels, and by **defacing** copies of famous works of art – for example, when Marcel Duchamp drew a moustache on the face of the Mona Lisa.

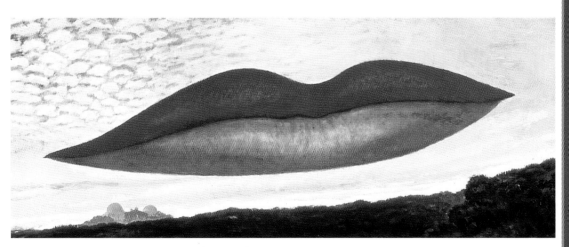

Observatory Time, by Man Ray (1932–34)
Man Ray described this work as two lips that were so large that they looked like two bodies – 'like the earth and sky, like you and me'. They also look like a strange UFO hovering above the earth.

Dada spread rapidly to Paris and New York and Cologne, in Germany. However, by 1919 it was beginning to collapse. In April 1920, Cologne Dada staged one of its most memorable exhibitions, which could only be entered through a public lavatory. This exhibition marks the transition from Dada to Surrealism and by the 1920s Dada had merged into Surrealism.

Two strands

Surrealism had two very distinct and different strands. One group of writers and painters, such as Joan Miró and André Masson, tried not to think of what they were writing or painting. They tried to stop the conscious part of their mind from working, and to let the pencil or brush simply take a walk in their hand to see what the unthinking or **unconscious** mind might produce. The works that they produced using this **automatic** technique look entirely **abstract** and bear no reference to the outside world of objects, people or landscapes.

The second group of artists, which includes Salvador Dalí, René Magritte and Paul Delvaux, painted very clear images of objects and landscapes, which we have no trouble in recognizing, except that these familiar objects and landscapes are placed in impossible settings, like pictures of dreams.

Lobster Telephone, by Salvador Dalí (1936)
Dalí placed a plaster lobster on this phone for the Surrealist apartment of his English patron Edward James. Dalí liked to suggest that when the handset was picked up it might bite.

Giorgio de Chirico 1888–1978

The Surrealists realized that certain artists showed 'surreal' qualities even before the term Surrealism existed. For example, the Italian artist Giorgio de Chirico's paintings showed dreamlike townscapes of deserted squares presented like a theatre set, framed by classical arches and columns. De Chirico was struck by the **futility** of life and the magic of objects. André Breton, the founder of Surrealism, listed de Chirico with Freud as one of the inspirations of Surrealism. Breton was first attracted to modern art by sighting de Chirico's *The Child's Brain* from a bus in 1913.

The Surrealists and war

Unlike some other art movements of the early 20th century, Surrealism did not grow directly out of the artists' and poets' reactions to war, but two leading members of the Surrealist movement, André Masson and Max Ernst, were both profoundly affected by their experience as soldiers in World War I (1914–18). Masson, who was badly wounded, became almost insane, experiencing vivid nightmares. Ernst claimed that the horrors and meaninglessness of war had made him 'a young man determined to find the myths of his time'.

Some of the Surrealists did produce works of art as a reaction to the horrors of war. Following the outbreak of the Spanish Civil War in 1936, Ernst tried to express his sense of helplessness in a painting called *The Angel of Heart and Home*, while Dali's *Autumn Cannibalism* depicts the cruelty of war through the shocking image of two creatures devouring each other. Later, the dropping of the atom bomb on the Japanese city of Hiroshima at the end of World War II had a profound impact on Dali's work. He began to paint exploded images, which seemed to have been shattered into several pieces.

The outbreak of World War II in 1939 marked a major change in the Surrealist movement. Most of the Surrealists left Paris, which was occupied by Nazi troops. Some artists returned to their native countries, but many escaped to the safety of America. Paris was no longer the centre of the art world and New York became the new heart of the Surrealist movement.

By the end of the war, the Surrealists were scattered, although many artists continued to create works in the Surrealist style throughout their lives.

Jean Arp 1887–1966

- Born 16 September 1887 in Strasbourg, Alsace-Lorraine, now in France.
- Died June 7 1966, Basel, Switzerland.

Key works

Birds in an Aquarium, c. 1920
Head: Scottish Lips, 1927
Garland of Buds, 1936

Arp was born Hans, but preferred to be known as Jean, the French form of his name. His family was wealthy – his father owned a cigar factory – and for the first few years of Arp's life, they lived in an old, 16th-century house.

Arp spent his entire childhood in Strasbourg. He was a dreamy child, keener on painting and poetry than on other school subjects. From an early age he wanted to be an artist, and later said that 'no other calling, no other profession was of interest to me'. He also said that it was 'probably the carvings on the cathedral of Strasbourg, my native city, which stimulated me to attempt sculpture'. At the age of ten he made two small wood carvings of Adam and Eve, inspired by the figures on the cathedral.

Feeling that his son was not working hard at school, Arp's father hired a private tutor for him and the two travelled to the mountainous region of the Vosges in France to work away from the distractions of the city. In the countryside around the Vosges, both student and tutor were more than happy to enjoy the pleasures of fishing, walking and reading poetry.

Eventually, Arp's tutor was dismissed and at the age of sixteen Arp became a student at the Strasbourg School of Arts and Crafts. There, he was so put off by the endless copying of stuffed birds and withered flowers that he decided to turn to poetry instead. Arp continued to write poetry throughout his life, even after he had become interested in art again.

Although he had been discouraged by his early experiences as an art student, by 1905 he started to study art again, but this time at the Weimar Academy in Germany. Arp studied at Weimar for two years and it was there that he had his first contact with contemporary French art. This led to his move to Paris at the age of 21 where he took more art classes.

■■■ *This photograph, taken in 1950, shows the artist at the age of 63 in a casual pose in his studio. It was taken two years after he resumed sculpture, which he had abandoned temporarily after the death of his wife and fellow artist Sophie Tauber.*

In 1908, Arp left Paris for Weggis in Switzerland where his father had settled. Here Arp went through a difficult period in his life. He later remembered it as a very lonely time when 'I never saw the least shadow of a man'. He read, drew and watched the snow clouds moving across the mountains. Arp was strongly influenced by the **abstract** shapes of the mountains and clouds around Weggis and it was at this time that he discovered abstract art. He met a group of Swiss artists and with them set up the Moderne Bund (Modern Group). During trips to Paris he became familiar with the work of Pablo Picasso and Georges Braque who were painting in the **Cubist** style.

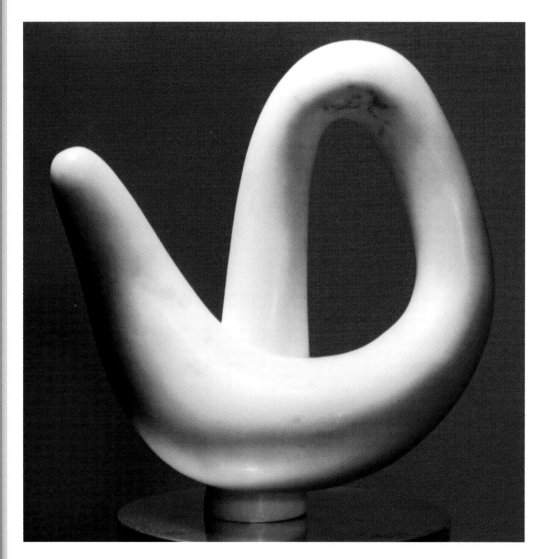

White Form, Jean Arp
Arp's work suggests the path of a plane looping through the sky, or the natural form of curiously shaped stone, washed smooth by lapping water.

During a visit to Germany, Arp met the Russian artist Wassily Kandinsky and several of **Der Blaue Reiter** (Blue Rider). The artists in this group painted colourful, almost abstract pictures, which were influenced by German and Russian folk art. Arp was invited to exhibit in the second Blaue Reiter exhibition in February 1912.

In 1914, Arp met Max Ernst in Cologne and recognized him as an artist with a similar sense of fantasy and invention to his own. After a brief spell in his home town of Strasbourg Arp returned to Paris where he met many artists and continued to develop his own style. However, when war broke out in 1914 Arp moved to Switzerland, which was neutral in the war.

In November 1915, Arp exhibited his **collages** and tapestries in Zurich. All of the works were abstract and none were traditional oil paintings on canvas. It was in Zurich that he met the Swiss artist Sophie Tauber. They fell in love at first sight and married in 1922. Together they experimented with collages made from wood, embroidery, cut-out paper, and pieces of newspaper, which, Arp explained, were all 'arranged according to the laws of chance'. Arp also wrote poems, taking words and phrases at random from newspapers and building them into his work.

In 1916, Arp was invited by a member of the **Dada** movement to take part in a cabaret – an artistic show involving art, music and poetry. He recited his own poetry and decorated the walls of the bar where the cabaret took place with coloured **reliefs** made from pieces of brightly painted wood. After this, Arp became very involved with the Dada movement, moving between the centres of Dada in Zurich and Cologne.

By the time the Arps settled in Paris in 1920 Dada was merging into Surrealism. Arp found himself associating with André Breton and the Surrealists. He took part in Surrealist exhibitions, making collages and reliefs out of pieces of wood and metal, using the effect of chance and coincidence as his inspiration. At the outbreak of World War II he and Sophie left Paris for Grasse in the South of France where they remained for nearly two years, living and working happily. By 1942 it was no longer safe to stay in France, so they returned to Zurich, where Sophie died the following year. This was a terrible blow to Arp. He created no sculpture for the following five years. However, Arp's last years were happy and productive. He continued to write poetry and work on his wood reliefs.

Salvador Dalí 1904–89

- Born 11 May 1904 in Figueras, Spain.
- Died 23 January 1989 in Torre Galatea, Spain.

Key works

The Persistence of Memory, 1931
Autumn Cannibalism, 1936
Metamorphosis of Narcissus, 1937
Lobster telephone (several versions)
Christ of St John of the Cross, 1951

The Spanish artist Salvador Dalí is the most famous of the Surrealists. He was christened Salvador after his elder brother who died in 1903. Dalí regularly saw his 'own' tombstone and felt he was accompanied by the spirit of his brother. Nearly four years later, his sister was born. Dalí's father was an **atheist**, but his mother was a devout Roman Catholic, and religious themes feature in his paintings. His artistic talent was evident from an early age – by the age of fourteen he was already holding exhibitions.

When he was sixteen, Dalí's mother died. In the same year he started at the Madrid School of Fine Arts where his teachers taught the **Post-Impressionist** style of painting. But Dalí admired the realistic style of the 17th-century painters Vermeer and Velasquez and wanted to be taught to paint like them. In 1923, he discovered the work of the Italian artist Giorgio de Chirico and his dreamlike but precise style influenced Dalí's work. Dalí was suspended from the art school for a year on a charge of urging students to rebel, and in 1926 he was permanently expelled. He explained that he had not sat his final exam because his teachers were not capable of judging his work.

In 1928, Dalí visited Paris. André Breton made him an official member of the Surrealist movement and wrote the introduction to the catalogue of an exhibition of Dalí's paintings. The exhibition attracted the attention of the artist René Magritte and the Surrealist poet Paul Eluard and his Russian-born wife, Gala. Dalí considered that his life changed when he met Gala. She became his partner, model and also his business manager. Gala was divorced from her husband in 1932 and married Dalí in 1934 in Paris.

In 1936, the Spanish Civil War began, and Dalí's *Autumn Cannibalism* mirrors two events – one political and one personal. The horror of the civil war is shown in his depiction of two creatures eating each other, but the painting also represents his and Gala's first kiss.

Dalí was a great showman in his dress and behaviour. He grew an immense moustache with waxed, curly ends which he called his antennae and claimed that these antennae allowed him to connect to **cosmic** forces. In 1936, he gave a lecture at the Surrealist exhibition in London wearing a diving suit, which nearly led to his death by suffocation. Dalí said he wanted to make paintings using snail shells filled with paint, drive elephants over the Pyrenees mountains, have his house guarded by rhinoceroses, and fill a Rolls-Royce with cauliflowers. Many people thought he was crazy, and Dalí played on this image of himself. He once declared, 'The only difference between a madman and me is that I am not mad.'

▮▮ *Salvador Dalí is shown with his trademark handlebar moustache, which he said, acted as antennae to cosmic forces. He points at a huge tome inscribed with his name, and stands in front of the St Peter's Basilica, as though to make a comparison with the greatness of the church, the book and the artist himself.*

Dalí's paintings often show highly detailed, imaginary or distorted figures and objects in impossible landscapes. Dalí painted the same things very often. Soft watches, crutches and ants often appear in his paintings, and the William Tell story, of a father who has to shoot an apple balanced on his son's head, is a favourite theme of Dalí's. Dalí made his life and surroundings surreal. He made surreal films and wrote two surreal versions of his life, *My Secret Life* and *Diary of a Genius*.

Dalí was fascinated by the way it is possible to see two objects in one shape, but not at the same time. He used this effect, which he called the paranoiac-critical method, in a number of works, such as *The Thought Machine* (1935).

Dalí was a great admirer of Freud and took his painting *Metamorphosis of Narcissus* to show him. Freud later wrote that he had always thought of the Surrealists as complete fools but he was impressed by Dalí's technical skill and '**fanatic** gaze'. Dalí made Freud think that it might be interesting to analyse a Surrealist painting.

In 1939, Breton expelled Dalí from the Surrealist movement because of his greed and cunningly rearranged the twelve letters of Dalí's name to form Avida Dollars, or 'greedy for dollars', a title that the artist happily adopted. That same year a New York department store **commissioned** Dalí to dress one of its windows. He created a disturbing Surrealist nightmare scene that attracted huge crowds and held up the traffic. The management removed some of the more outrageous exhibits. But Dalí then climbed into the display, smashed the window with a bathtub and soaked the amazed onlookers. Dalí was arrested, but he later justified himself on the grounds that every artist has the right to defend his work to the limit.

In 1940, Dalí and Gala left Europe for the USA where they remained throughout World War II, and where Gala calmly organized everything for Dalí's comfort. The dropping of the atom bomb on Hiroshima in Japan profoundly shocked Dalí. From this point on he began to paint exploded images, and also included religious imagery in his paintings.

In 1948, Dalí and Gala returned to Europe. During this period, Dalí painted a number of works which feature Gala as the Madonna, and several portraits of Christ, including his famous *Christ of St John of the Cross*.

Dalí was an incredibly versatile artist. As well as paintings, he made jewellery, glassware, clothes and tableware, and also directed films, opera, ballet and theatrical performances. In 1929, he worked with his friend the Spanish film maker Luis Buñuel to create the Surrealist film *Un Chien Andalou*. He wrote a screenplay for the Marx brothers and created a giant painting of bulbous eyeballs for the set of Alfred Hitchcock's film *Spellbound*. Dalí designed Surrealist interiors including chairs, tables, lamps, a lobster telephone and a shocking pink sofa in the shape of the lips of the famous film star Mae West.

In 1982, Gala died. Dalí fell into depression and tried to commit suicide by refusing to drink any liquids. Even this act was surreal, because he believed that if he became dehydrated (completely dried out) he would be immortal, and then a drop of liquid could bring him back to life later. He became unable to swallow and had to be fed by liquids through his nose for the rest of his life. He moved to the castle at Pubol in Spain, which he had given to Gala, and continued to work. In 1984, he suffered severe burns in a fire and finally died of heart failure at the age of 84.

■■ *The Persistence of Memory*, by Salvador Dalí (1931)
Dalí frequently painted soft watches drooping on branches or from tables, contradicting the very nature of what we expect from a timepiece.

Paul Delvaux 1897–1994

- Born 23 September 1897 in Anheit, Belgium.
- Died 20 July 1994 in Veurne, Belgium.

Key works
Dawn over the City, 1940
Sleeping Venus, 1944
A Mermaid in Full Moonlight, 1949

Paul Delvaux was the elder of two boys. His father was a lawyer who insisted that his sons should have a good education. Delvaux studied Greek and Latin at high school in Brussels. He discovered the work of the Greek poet Homer, and made many drawings of subjects from Greek mythology – a source of inspiration for him throughout his life. Although he really wanted to study to become a painter, he agreed to study architecture in order to please his family. In 1916, he enrolled in the school of architecture at the Brussels Academy of Fine Arts, but later he changed to the painting school.

Photographed here towards the end of his very long life (he died in his 97th year) we see Delvaux standing in front of one of his own paintings. His style remained almost unchanged throughout his lifetime.

Between 1920 and 1921, Delvaux served his **military service**, attending evening classes taught by the Belgian **Symbolist** painter Jean Deville at the Academy of Brussels. In 1922, he painted his first railway station – the first of many trains in his work, which feature as symbols of memory and childhood. 'As a child I liked trains and this nostalgia has stayed with me; memories of youth ... I paint the trains of childhood and consequently, that childhood itself.'

In 1926, he first saw the work of the Italian painter Giorgio de Chirico and was deeply impressed by its haunting, dreamlike quality. He realized that this was the kind of mood he too wished to create. Delvaux called de Chirico 'the poet of emptiness'. He admired his empty town squares and menacing shadows.

Around 1930, Delvaux visited a fair and saw a display that was to have a profound effect on his work. In fact his account of what he saw could be a description of many of his own works: 'I went to the Brussels fair where I was struck by the extraordinary Spitzner Museum booth, with its red velvet display window, two skeletons and a mechanical sleeping Venus made from papier maché. There was something strange and sad about it in the middle of the hubbub of the carousels, of that blustering false gaiety that characterizes these large fairs.'

From this point on, Delvaux's work had a Surrealist feel, which was to develop even more strongly after he saw the work of the Surrealists in 1934. In 1936, he exhibited his paintings with his fellow countryman René Magritte in Brussels, and in 1938 his works were included in an international Surrealist exhibition in Paris.

In 1952, Delvaux married Anne-Marie de Maertelaere, a woman he had known for 32 years. From 1950 to 1960 he taught at the School of Art and Architecture in Brussels and in 1965 he became the director of Belgium's Academy of Fine Arts.

Delvaux's paintings show surprising encounters in unexpected places. The classical temple, the train, the skeleton and the naked goddess are constant **motifs** in his paintings. His style changed very little throughout his long life. On his 90th birthday there were exhibitions of his work in Belgium, France, Switzerland and Japan. He died in Belgium in 1994.

Nuit de Noel (Christmas Eve), by Paul Delvaux (1956)
The title makes us wonder at the poetic significance of a girl, seen from behind, and standing alone on an empty station platform, lit, like the pylons and train carriage by the light of the full moon.

19

Marcel Duchamp 1887–1968

- Born 28 July 1887 in Blainville, France.
- Died 2 October 1968 in Paris, France.

Key works
The Large Glass, 1915–23
Fountain, 1917
L.H.O.O.Q., 1919

Marcel Duchamp was one of six children. Four of them became well-known artists, and some of them agreed to use different surnames. The eldest was the painter Jacques Villon. After him came Raymond Duchamp-Villon, a sculptor. Marcel Duchamp was eleven years younger than Raymond and their sister Suzanne – also a painter – was two years younger than Marcel.

▐ *This photograph of Marcel Duchamp – one of the most influential artists of the 20th century – was taken when he was 64. His ready-mades and theories of art played a vital role in the development of 20th-century art.*

Duchamp's father was a lawyer who allowed his children to choose their own careers, but did not give them a lot of money. In 1904, Duchamp left for Paris where he lived with his brother, Jacques Villon. He described this time as 'eight years of swimming lessons' during which he experimented with painting styles and techniques. He also trained as a librarian, and worked for a while as an illustrator for a French newspaper, as well as supporting himself by teaching French.

In 1911, Duchamp joined the **Section d'Or** group, a group of **Cubist** painters, and exhibited his paintings with them, showing his *Nude Descending a Staircase* based on photographs of a human figure walking down stairs. In the same year Duchamp finished his pamphlet, *Journey Around Painting in Eight Months*. From this point on he turned his back on traditional art.

In 1913, Duchamp declared that Cubism was a dead end, and that he was abandoning painting altogether. That year he created his first **ready-mades**. These were **found objects** which, according to Duchamp, became works of art simply by being selected by an artist. By exhibiting his ready-mades as art, Duchamp was making the statement that art is anything the artist says it is. This was a **radical** statement, which has had an immense impact on the art of the 20th century. His first exhibited ready-made – a bottle rack – was shown to the public in 1914, and was followed by *Fountain*. *Fountain* is a urinal, signed 'R. Mutt' by Duchamp, and dated 1917. It was rejected by the Salon des

Indépendants, an important art exhibition in Paris, on the grounds that it was not art but plumbing, to which Duchamp replied, 'Whether Mr Mutt with his own hands made the fountain or not has no importance. He CHOSE it. He took an ordinary article of life, placed it so that its usual significance disappeared under the new title and point of view – created a new object for thought for that object.'

In 1915, Duchamp went to America where he helped to start up the New York **Dada** movement. Duchamp was a great influence on the **innovative** American photographer Alfred Stieglitz. He also edited magazines, such as *Wrong-Wrong* and *The Blind Man*, and made experimental films. Later, Duchamp also played a part in setting up Surrealism. In 1941, he organized a large Surrealist exhibition in New York, and became co-editor with André Breton and Max Ernst of the Surrealist New York magazine, *VVV*.

Duchamp was a Dadaist who made his most important work before the birth of Surrealism in 1924. However, he still had a huge influence on the Surrealist movement.

▌▌ *Fountain*, by Marcel Duchamp (1917)
  This is one of the landmark works in the history of 20th-century art: not made by the artist but found, signed with an invented name, and exhibited. It presents a challenge to what we expect of an artwork and makes a statement that art is anything the artist says it is.

Max Ernst 1891–1976

- Born 2 April 1891 in Brühl, Germany.
- Died 1 April 1976 in Paris, France.

Key works
Of This Men Shall Know Nothing, 1923
Pietà or Revolution by Night, 1923
Two Children Menaced by a Nightingale, 1924

Ernst was one of seven children. He was born the year after his older sister, Maria, died at the age of six. This fact had a profound affect on Ernst and he later gave a poetic description of his birth: 'On 2 April at 9.45 a.m., Max Ernst hatched from the egg which his mother had laid in an eagle's nest and over which the bird had brooded for seven years.' This description reflects the important role that birds played in his imagination. He gave himself a bird identity, calling himself 'Loplop, Bird Superior', and included this bird in many of his paintings and drawings.

Ernst later described his parents: 'My father Philipp Ernst was by profession a teacher of deaf mutes, by vocation a painter, authoritarian, well-built, a devout Catholic, always in a good mood. My mother Luise ... was loving, with a good sense of humour and supply of fairy tales.' The fairy tales that his mother told him had a profound effect on the artist's imagination.

Following his parents' wishes, Ernst enrolled at Bonn University in 1909. Here he studied philosophy, psychiatry and art history. He was drawn to the art of the insane and began to study the drawings of mental patients. Although he was interested in art he carefully avoided any art course that would teach him how to paint in order to earn a living. He was not interested in learning how to paint 'properly' but in painting as a way to express a mood, such as desire or menace.

In 1911, Ernst met the painter Auguste Macke, co-founder of the German **Der Blaue Reiter** group, and in 1913 he began to exhibit his work with them. He was attracted by the way the group used colour to express emotions.

When war broke out in 1914, Ernst joined a gunners' regiment as an engineer and was powerfully affected by his experiences. He wrote later: 'How to overcome the disgust and fatal boredom that military life and the horrors of war create? Howl? Blaspheme? Vomit?' After the war ended, he saw the beginning of a new life, and wrote: 'On 1 August 1914 Max Ernst died. He was resurrected on 11 November 1918 as a young man who aspired to find the myths of his time.'

Ernst was strikingly handsome. He became an important figure in the Cologne group of **Dada** artists, working under the name Dadamax. In October 1918, he married Luise Strauss, a university student studying art history, and two years later they had a son, Jimmy. In 1921, Ernst was visited in Cologne by the poet Paul Eluard, one of the founder members of the Surrealist movement. Ernst fell in love with Eluard's wife, Gala (who later became Dalí's wife), left his wife Luise and moved to Paris, where he lived with Eluard and Gala. In Paris he also met André Breton, the founder of Surrealism.

Ernst had started making **collages** in 1919. By 1921, Ernst was already painting surreal images such as *The Elephant Celebes*, and in 1923, he painted one of the first Surrealist masterpieces, *Of This Men Shall Know Nothing,* and dedicated it to Breton.

Portrait of Ernst, by Hans Bellmer
The German artist Bellmer painted the face of Ernst as though part of a mosaic, fractured and then reassembled.

Breton urged Ernst not to think about what he was making but to start with something accidental. This happened quite naturally when Ernst was staying at an inn by the sea one rainy day and began to stare at the wooden floor. Hypnotized by what he saw, Ernst took paper and pencil and began to make rubbings of the floorboards, moving the paper at random and finding he had created a strange, visionary world from these rubbings. He continued his experiments by rubbing paper or canvas on tree bark, making a trail of smoke using a candle, and smudging a blob of paint on his canvas. He said that by making art this way he was a 'spectator at the birth of all my works', suggesting that the works made themselves and were not the deliberate creation of an artist.

The technique of rubbing which Ernst developed from 1925 onwards is called by its French name, frottage. It became Ernst's favourite technique: 'at random I drop pieces of paper on the floor and then rub them with black lead'. These textured images were then arranged to form a **collage**.

Der Rosa Vogel (The Pink Bird), by Max Ernst (1956)
Much of Ernst's work includes bird imagery, and the artist described himself as Loplop, the bird superior. It also shows his use of frottage – rubbing against grains of trees and bark to produce a texture, which is then worked into the image.

Ernst's first frottages were published in 1925 as a work called *Natural History*. Four years later he published a book of collages. Ernst was also interested in memory, dream and chance, and while some of his images began with random rubbings, he also painted clear images of disturbing and puzzling scenes.

In 1926, Ernst met the 18-year-old Marie-Berthe Aurenche. After divorcing his first wife he married Marie-Berthe in 1927. The same year he created his *Forest Series*. These were paintings made from bark rubbings which resembled a dense wood. Ernst describes the 'enchantment and terror' he had felt the first time his father took him into a forest.

Ernst created disturbing collages by cutting out Victorian images and rearranging them to create sinister and provocative works. One of the most famous of these showed two women holding hands on a sofa while a reptile climbed over one them. By introducing surreal and disturbing images into Victorian interiors he turned scenes of polite conversation into a nightmare world of horror and disgust.

Ernst had romantic affairs with the Surrealist artists Meret Oppenheim, Léonor Fini and Leonora Carrington, and in 1936 he divorced Marie-Berthe. After a quarrel with Breton, Ernst left the Surrealist group in Paris and headed for the South of France. At the outbreak of World War II in 1939, Ernst was placed under arrest because he was a German citizen, and escaped from several camps. He had met Peggy Guggenheim, the wealthy American collector and patron of the arts, and in 1941 he married her and settled in the USA, away from the horrors of war in Europe.

In 1942, Ernst met the artist Dorothea Tanning and divorced Peggy Guggenheim. In 1946 he married Tanning in Beverly Hills. It was a double wedding with Man Ray who married Juliet Browner. Ernst and Tanning lived in Sedona, Arizona before returning to Europe in 1950. Towards the end of his life, his works became increasingly colourful and **abstract**. He died in Paris at the age of 85.

Alberto Giacometti 1901–66

- Born 10 October 1901 in Borgonovo, Switzerland.
- Died 11 January 1966 in Chur, Switzerland.

Key works
Suspended Ball, 1930–31
The Cage, 1930–31
Woman with her Throat Cut, 1932
Three Figures Outdoors, 1929

Alberto Giacometti was born in a small mountain village in the Italian-speaking part of Switzerland. He was the eldest of four children. His father, Giovanni, was a **Post-Impressionist** painter who owned works by Cézanne and van Gogh.

Giacometti described his early years as very happy: 'I cannot imagine a happier childhood and adolescence than my own, spent with my father and the rest of my family, my mother and sister and brothers.' At the age of twelve he painted his first picture – a still-life of apples, and the following year made his first sculpture, a bust of his brother Diego.

Giacometti studied art and sculpture in Geneva, Switzerland. When he was eighteen, he accompanied his father to Venice in Italy, where he was profoundly impressed by the work of the 16th-century Venetian painter Titian. He returned to Italy to study, mainly in Rome, and stayed there until he was 20.

In 1922, Giacometti travelled to Paris where he was to live for the rest of his life. At first, he worked in the studio of the **Cubist** sculptor Alexander Archipenko until Archipenko moved to New York in 1923. On his father's instructions, he began attending classes with the sculptor Antoine Bourdelle, who worked in the traditional, **representational** style. Giacometti worked with Bourdelle for five years. During these years he spent a lot of time studying the works in the Louvre gallery and also became friendly with other young artists in Paris. In 1925, he saw work by Jean Arp and Constantin Brancusi. This encouraged him to move away from traditional sculpture and towards a flatter, more **abstract** style. At about this time, his brother Diego joined him in Paris. Diego became a skilled metal-worker, and worked as Alberto's assistant.

In 1927, the two brothers rented a small studio. It was cramped, uncomfortable and run-down, but this was where Giacometti worked and lived until his death 39 years later. To support themselves, he and Diego made furniture and objects, and jewellery for the designer Elsa Schiaparelli.

■■ *Giacometti at work on a sculpture in 1958. Here we see the sculptor in suit, shirt and tie, in his Paris studio modelling the clay to form the stretched head and shoulders of a figure.*

■▮ *The Couple*, by Alberto Giacometti (1926–27)
*The title of this sculpture urges us to see it not as an **abstract** work
but as a stylized representation of female and male. The smaller
figure contains female body parts above legs and feet, the taller figure
is read as a male only in context with its partner.*

Meret Oppenheim 1913–85

Meret Oppenheim was born in Germany and studied art in Basel, Switzerland. She moved to Paris in 1932 where she met Giacometti and Arp. Through them she was introduced to the Surrealists. She became known as the ultimate Surrealist woman, a child-woman, who because of her youth, innocence and charm seemed to have a direct connection to childhood and the world of dreams. The Surrealists called her 'the fairy woman whom all men desire'. She first exhibited with them in 1933, and continued to take part in meetings and exhibitions until 1937. Her fur-lined cup and saucer, which makes two practical and useful objects entirely useless, has become one of the most memorable Surrealist images.

Giacometti joined the Surrealist movement in 1930, taking part in the group's exhibitions and activities. His work was praised by Dalí, who was especially enthusiastic about Giacometti's sculpture *Suspended Ball*. For five years Giacometti was Surrealism's most **innovative** sculptor, but in 1935 he began studying live models again and returned to **representational** art. He rejected Surrealism and stopped exhibiting his work. This was the start of many years of mental struggle and self-doubt, and he did not exhibit his work again until 1947.

In 1938, Giacometti was hit by a car. His foot was crushed and he was in hospital for many months. The accident had a profound effect on him and for a long while he could not work. However, in 1940, he began to work again, but this time working not from models but from memory. His figures shrank to a very small size.

Giacometti spent most of World War II in Switzerland, which remained neutral during the war. For four years he lived in a hotel room in Geneva, returning after the war to his Paris studio, which his brother Diego had looked after for him. He took his work back to Paris in six matchboxes. In 1949, at the age of 48, he married Annette Arm who he had met seven years earlier and who had been the model for many of his works.

By the end of his life, Giacometti had become famous, with exhibitions held in Europe and the USA, but despite his success he never lost his self-doubt. He died from cancer at the age of 64 and was buried in Borgonovo, the village of his birth.

Frida Kahlo 1907–54

- Born on 6 July 1907 in Mexico City, Mexico.
- Died on 2 July 1954 in Mexico.

Key works
The Two Fridas, 1939
Self-portrait with Monkey, 1940
Self-portrait with Hair Cut Off, 1940

Frida Kahlo was the daughter of a devout Catholic Mexican mother and a German-Jewish father who had emigrated to Mexico when he was nineteen and earned a living as a photographer. She was one of six girls – with three sisters and two half-sisters from her father's first marriage. The Kahlos lived in a comfortable family house, known as the 'Blue House', in the historic district of Mexico City.

Three years before Kahlo was born, a revolution took place in Mexico which overthrew the old right-wing government. In later life, Kahlo maintained that she was born in 1910. She did this not simply to appear younger than she was, but also to be a true daughter of the Mexican Revolution – born into a new and liberated country.

At the age of six, Kahlo caught polio, a very serious disease, and had to stay in bed for almost a year. Her illness left her with one leg shorter than the other and this led to taunts from her classmates at school. Too proud to show how much this upset her, she retreated into the world of her imagination.

When she was still very young, Kahlo's father trained her to use a camera and develop film. She was his favourite child. 'Frida is my most intelligent daughter. She's most like me,' he boasted. In 1922 Kahlo began studying at university in Mexico City. She planned to become a doctor, but her life changed dramatically in 1925 when she had a terrible accident. The coach on which she regularly returned home was hit by a tram. The impact broke her pelvis, shattered her spine and shoulder blades, broke her right leg in eleven places and entirely crushed her right foot. This terrible accident caused her to abandon her studies and she was forced to accept the fact that she would be an invalid for the rest of her life. While she lay in bed she began to paint pictures of her family and friends and devour books on art history. A year after the accident, she painted her first self-portrait.

Four years after her accident, at the age of 22, Kahlo married the 43-year-old Mexican artist Diego Rivera. Rivera painted **murals** on left-wing political themes and was the most famous artist in the country. Frida accompanied him to San Francisco in the USA where he worked from 1930 to 1933. During this time, she began to work on her own painting, and completed a dozen works before returning to Mexico. In San Francisco, Frida met Dr Leo Eloesser who became her doctor and lifelong friend and who discovered that her spine was crooked. The foot that had been damaged in her accident was also painful and she found it increasingly difficult to walk. But most painful of all to Kahlo was the discovery that she was unable to have children, and her longing for a baby is reflected in many of her paintings.

▮▮ Self-portrait, by Frida Kahlo (1930)
Kahlo frequently painted herself in a way that shows her looking far less lovely than she appears in photographs. She often wears jewellery, hairstyle and costume that reflect her Mexican identity.

Kahlo and Rivera supported left-wing politics. Rivera spent ten months in Moscow in 1927–28 and took part in the 10th anniversary of the **October Revolution**. In January 1937, the Russian revolutionary leader, Leon Trotsky, was expelled from the USSR. Rivera asked the Mexican president for permission to receive Trotsky in Mexico and Kahlo welcomed Trotsky and his wife at the airport and took them to the Blue House, where they lived rent-free for two years. During this time, Kahlo and Trotsky had a passionate affair.

In 1939, André Breton and his wife came to Mexico and met the Riveras and the Trotskys. Breton was a great admirer of Kahlo's work and urged her to exhibit in Paris. Kahlo agreed and was a big success in France. The Louvre Museum bought one of her works and Pablo Picasso, who greatly admired her, presented her with a pair of earrings in the shape of two hands, which she often wore.

Viva la Vida (Long Live Life), by Frida Kahlo (1954)
The title of this work is inscribed on a piece of cut melon in the foreground. Painted in the year of her death, after much pain and suffering, it is a poignant statement of what she knew she was shortly to lose.

Kahlo returned to Mexico in 1940 where she remarried Rivera from whom she had separated on 6 November 1939. From this time on, she stayed in the Blue House, painting and teaching with Rivera, and becoming increasingly weak physically. She had to spend a lot of time in bed, and to wear a steel body brace. She had a serious operation on her spine in New York in 1946, and underwent seven more spinal operations, spending a whole year bedridden in hospital in Mexico City in 1950. She became increasingly fragile, but whether in bed at home or in hospital, she continued to paint. She arrived at her first solo exhibition at the Gallery of Contemporary Art in Mexico City in an ambulance and was carried in on a stretcher to a four-poster bed, becoming part of her exhibition on suffering.

Shortly before Kahlo's death, it was necessary to amputate her right leg which had become infected with gangrene. She died in the Blue House, aged 47. Her body was placed in Mexican dress in the Palace of Fine Arts and hundreds of mourners came to pay their last respects.

Leonora Carrington b. 1917

While she was an art student in London, Leonora Carington had an affair with Max Ernst, which led to her association with the Surrealists. At the outbreak of World War II, Ernst had to return to Germany and Carrington moved to Spain, where she had a nervous breakdown and received treatment in a private clinic. In 1941, she married the Mexican poet Renato Leduc and the following year they moved to Mexico where she devoted herself to painting. Here she developed her personal style, which featured elements from her own life and **occult** themes. Carrington divorced Leduc and married the Hungarian photographer Imre Weisz in 1946. She remained committed to Surrealism throughout her life. Her work is full of animals and personal imagery, and is often terrifying.

René Magritte 1898–1967

- Born 21 November 1898 in Lessines, Belgium.
- Died 15 August 1967 in Brussels.

Key works
The Assassin Threatened, 1926
The Lovers, 1928
Red Model, 1935

René Magritte was the eldest of three brothers. The family was comfortably off – Magritte's father was a manufacturer and a trader – and they moved around Belgium a great deal during his childhood, before settling in Brussels when Magritte was 20.

When he was eight years old Magritte had an experience that led directly to his wish to become an artist. Playing in an abandoned cemetery with a young girl he saw an artist painting, and was struck by painting as a magical activity. From the age of ten, Magritte took private lessons in painting. It was the 'magical' and disquieting aspect of art and life he responded to. His earliest memory was of a crate next to his cradle, which seemed to him very mysterious. He was also fascinated by aspects of religion such as priests' vestments, the smell of incense, church music and relics. He dressed up as a priest and held private masses in front of a home-made altar.

In 1912 a traumatic event struck the family. His mother, who suffered from depression, committed suicide by drowning. Her dead and bloated body was found three weeks later and brought back to the house where it remained in a downstairs room. Her nightdress had risen to cover her head, and the imagery of the female figure with a veiled head frequently appears in his work, for example in *The Heart of the Matter* and *The Lovers*.

Magritte was very close to his brother Paul. Both were very interested in the arts – painting, music, literature and the cinema. Magritte was keen on a scary crime series with a sinister and mysterious hero.

From 1916 to 1918, Magritte studied at the Academy of Fine Arts in Brussels. After completing his **military service**, he returned to Brussels, where he supported himself financially by working as a designer of posters and publicity material, and by painting large roses in a wallpaper factory.

■■ René Magritte is shown here looking deliberately more like a businessman than an artist. Unlike the flamboyant Salvador Dalí, he maintained a serious composure and manner throughout his life.

Magritte first saw the beautiful Georgette Berger from a carousel at the annual town fair in Charleroi when he was fifteen. He met her again by chance in the Botanic Gardens in Brussels, and they got married in 1922. Georgette remained his model throughout his life.

In 1922, Magritte met the poet Marcel Lecomte, who showed him Giorgio de Chirico's painting *The Song of Love*. The impact on Magritte was immense: 'de Chirico showed me that the most important thing was to know what to paint.' Magritte was fascinated by the mystery of de Chirico's work, but it was not until three years later that he made his first decisively Surrealist work. *The Two Sisters* painted in 1925 shows a double portrait of a girl viewed by day and by night. The model was his wife Georgette.

In the summer of 1927, the Magrittes moved to Perreux-sur-Marne, near Paris where Magritte's dealer Camille Goemans was living. Goemans' gallery

The Lovers, by René Magritte (1928)
The veiled heads of the two lovers remind us of the artist's drowned mother found with her nightdress covering her face. The veiled head was an image the artist used often. A dreamlike snapshot is presented by the image of these veiled lovers who can not see each other and can not properly kiss one another.

exhibited works by the Surrealists, and through him they met the Surrealist poets André Breton and Paul Eluard. This was a very fruitful time for Magritte and he created some of his finest paintings during his stay in Paris. However, he disliked certain Surrealist practices such as **automatism**. He also disliked Breton's strong anti-Catholic views. In 1930, Magritte became very angry when Breton criticized Georgette for wearing a cross – a family heirloom – around her neck. Soon after Magritte and Georgette left Paris and returned to settle permanently in Brussels.

Magritte hated travelling, and remained in Belgium after his return from Paris. He lived an ordered and regular life. He took a morning walk with his dog Loulou to buy food for the day. He spent the afternoon in a cafe, and enjoyed the companionship of gatherings of friends on Sundays. His house was deliberately middle-class, furnished with comfortable sofas and chairs and a baby grand piano. Interestingly he did not have a studio but painted in the dressing room next to his bedroom. He had always worked like this – in the kitchen or dining room with a single easel and a few paints, brushes and charcoal – neatly and tidily.

Magritte did not like showy clothes or behaviour. Instead he preferred anonymity and wore a sober suit, overcoat and bowler hat. A story is told of how his wife invited a couple to their house for a cup of coffee. While the women were in the kitchen leaving the two men together, Magritte approached the man from behind and kicked him hard on the bottom. The man turned, outraged at the act, but Magritte continued as though nothing had happened, forcing the man to wonder if this was a figment of his imagination, a thought made impossible by the pain in his backside. This completely unexpected act was a deliberately Surrealist gesture.

In 1938, Magritte took part in the International Surrealist Exhibition in Paris. His images present dreamlike scenes, which create a feeling of anxiety or panic. Men in bowler hats, naked women and steam trains often appear in his paintings, as do words, which add a further puzzling dimension to the work.

Magritte enjoyed the visual result of placing together objects and figures have no relationship to each other. His paintings make things that we know and are familiar with seem strange by changing their scale and putting them in unexpected places. Like Dalí, Magritte was interested in the way a single shape can look like two entirely different things.

Magritte died at the age of 68. His paintings did not gain very much recognition during his lifetime, but after his death they became hugely popular. His style remained almost unchanged through his life.

André Masson 1896–1987

- Born 4 January 1896 in Balagny-sur-Thérin, France.
- Died 28 October 1987 in Paris.

Key works

Battle of Fishes, 1926
Children of the Island, 1926–7
Ariadne's Thread, 1938
Gradiva, 1939

Masson did not like to discuss his childhood. He wanted to exist purely in the present, and not be made up of events from his past. We know, however, that he was born on 4 January 1896 at Balagny, Oise, France, and that he studied art in Brussels and later in Paris.

Masson travelled in Italy and Switzerland before serving as a soldier in World War I. He was severely wounded when a bullet ripped through his chest. Masson later described how he felt after he was wounded. He said that the world around him seemed full of wonder, and the sky seemed like a body of light. He remained standing, unaware of the pain, and had to be pulled out of danger by a fellow soldier. Then he had to wait for help until nightfall when the stretcher-bearers arrived. He lay in a cramped hole beside the dead body of a German soldier who he would later refer to as Rameses II, because the soldier seemed to be mummified, like an Egyptian pharoah.

In hospital, Masson refused treatment, raging and screaming until he was finally sent to a psychiatric hospital. Here he yearned for far-off places like the Indies, away from the horrors of war in Europe. At the end of the war in 1918, he was shattered and damaged, and on the brink of insanity.

In 1922, Masson moved to Paris where he became friendly with Joan Miró, and made his action paintings. In these works he tried to let the **unconscious** part of his brain take over and create paintings that were the result of spontaneous, unthinking action. While he was in Paris, Masson became involved with André Breton and Paul Eluard and joined the Surrealists, taking part in their exhibitions. He became an important figure in French art.

▍▍ *André Masson, late in life, in the comfort of his living room in Paris.*

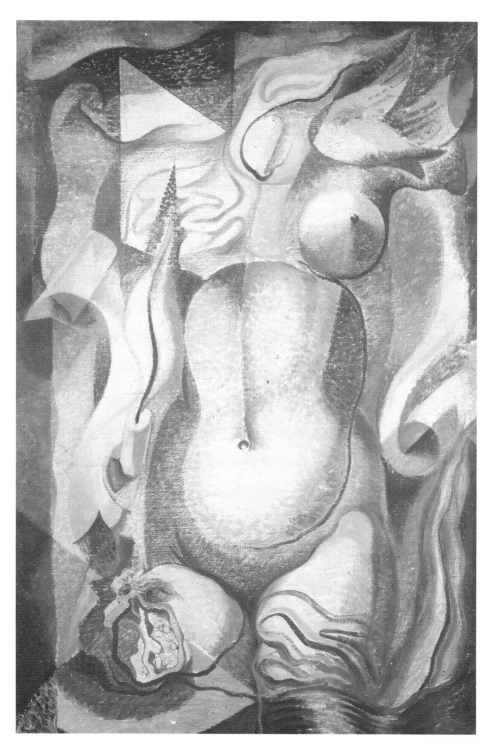

■■ *Armour*, by André Masson

This fragmented image of a figure has no head or limbs. Masson shows us only a body and the suggestion of a severed leg. The work seems representative of his sufferings during World War I.

Eileen Agar 1904-91

Agar was born in Argentina, South America, but she moved to London to study at the Slade School of Art. Later she studied in Paris and met the Surrealists. Her work was selected by Roland Penrose for the International Surrealist Exhibition in London in 1936. From 1936 she experimented with automatic techniques of painting and drawing developed by André Masson. Agar also made sculptures using shells and starfish, and tried out new materials, such as fabric over plaster. Her most famous work is probably the *Angel of Anarchy*, a plaster cast of a male head, draped in silk and beads, which she created in 1936.

Masson quarrelled with Breton in 1929 and broke with the Surrealists. In 1934, he moved to Catalonia in Spain where he remained until the outbreak of the Spanish Civil War in 1936. He returned to France in 1937, renewed his friendship with Breton and entered his second Surrealist phase, but as the horrors of World War II tore through Europe, he left for the islands of Martinique and the Antilles, eventually arriving in the USA.

Masson lived in or near New York City from 1941 until the end of World War II. His **automatic** painting, in which he often used glue and sand, or squeezed paint onto canvas directly from the tube had a great impact on the Abstract Expressionist artists Arshile Gorky, Jackson Pollock and Mark Rothko. Masson believed that the act of painting should be swift and automatic and use the whole body. He said that artists should lay their canvas on the floor and see the canvas as a '**cosmic** space' without a centre or any landmarks. He also told artists to think of creation as 'a risk to be taken' and urged them to see their paintings as 'a commitment and an adventure'.

After the war Masson returned to France where he lived in Paris and Aix-en-Provence until 1955. He travelled frequently, living in Venice and Rome for short periods. In 1965 he received an important **commission** to paint the ceiling of the Théâtre de l'Odéon in Paris. Despite his early experiences of physical and mental wounds during World War I, Masson survived until the age of 81, dying in Paris in October 1987.

Joan Miró 1893–1983

- Born 20 April 1893 in Barcelona, Spain.
- Died 25 December 1983 in Palma, Mallorca.

Key works
The Harlequin's Carnival, 1924
Person Throwing a Stone at a Bird, 1926
Dog Barking at the Moon, 1926

Miró was born in the historic heart of old Barcelona, the son of a goldsmith. He was a sickly child with a poor appetite, so his parents sent him to live with his grandparents in the country.

At the age of fourteen Miró joined the School of Fine Arts in Barcelona. Although he had a very sensitive response to colour he was not good at drawing and he failed his exams. His father insisted he give up his training as a painter to study at the School of Commerce, which he did for three years, and failed there too. He became ill and depressed, suffered a mental collapse, and then caught typhoid. Fearing that their son would die, Miró's parents sent him to Montroig, where the family spent their summers, and here he began to recover.

Miró persuaded his parents to allow him to enter Francesco Gali's School of Art in Barcelona in 1912. To help his drawing technique his first teacher made him draw objects that he could touch because Miró seemed only able to see lines and colour. His early pictures are landscapes and portraits that combine the style of his native Spanish folk art with strong, bright colour. He also adopted a **Cubist** style for a short while, but between 1918 and 1922 he developed an individual style, which was deliberately primitive and highly detailed.

In 1917, Miró had his first exhibition, but because his paintings were not traditional, finished works his exhibition aroused a great deal of anger and cruel remarks. Miró was even viewed as a madman (a term that André Breton considered the greatest compliment). In 1919, Miró made the first of many visits to Paris, and the following year he settled there, becoming part of an **avant-garde** circle of artists and joining in the meetings of the Paris **Dadaists**. He lived next door to André Masson and through him met the Surrealists, and was invited to take part in their first group show in 1925.

Self–portrait, by Joan Miró (1919)
Miró was friends with many Surrealist and **abstract** painters, including Picasso,
Masson and Ernst, but he never fully accepted the movement's beliefs and
refused to sign the Surrealist **Manifesto**.

Breton described Miró as 'the most surrealist of us all'. This may have had something to do with the artist's poverty and lack of food. Miró said that hunger and staring at the cracks in the wall made him hallucinate (see things that are not really there), which helped him to paint unusual and strange forms.

Miró created **automatic** paintings, without any planning or thought beforehand. One critic described Miró's painting method in the following way: 'Miró no longer prepares his paintings; he gives them not the slightest thought in the world before taking brush or pencil in hand ... The forms install themselves on the canvas without a preconceived idea. He begins them by spilling a little colour on the surface and then circulates a dipped brush around the canvas. As his hand moves the obscure vision becomes more precise.'

Miró tried to free his **unconscious**, to let his emotions take over, and paint in a childlike state. 'I paint in the room where I was born,' said Miró. He maintained that although his works looked **abstract** they always represented something: 'For me a form is never something abstract, it is always the sign of something. It is always a man, a bird or something else. For me a painting is never form for form's sake.'

A visit to Belgium and Holland in 1928 exposed him to the work of the Dutch Old Masters, especially Vermeer, which affected his style. He painted his *Dutch Interiors* and created several sculptures and **collages** during this period. In 1929, he married Pilar Juncosa in Majorca, and returned with her to Paris, and the following year his only child, Dolores, was born. In 1932, he moved back to his childhood home in Barcelona, and designed the costumes and sets for the Ballets Russes production of *Jeux d'enfants*.

When the Spanish Civil War broke out in July 1936, Miró left for London and then Paris where his family joined him the following month. He was to remain in France until 1940. At first, without a home or a studio, he was unable to paint, and instead kept a journal in which he wrote poetry and prose. In 1937, he painted a giant **mural** for the Spanish Pavillion at the Paris World Fair – a powerful image of a farmer holding a sickle. He also designed a poster to support the Spanish struggle in which he showed a huge figure clenching his upraised fist in a gesture of freedom. In 1940, Miró returned to Spain to escape the horrors of German-occupied France during World War II.

During the 1940s Miró produced a broad range of graphic work. He is often seen as the most fun-loving and joyful of the Surrealists. In 1947, he travelled for the first time to the USA where he created a huge mural for the Terrace

Plaza Hotel in Cincinnati. He also produced a painting for the Stanhope Hotel in New York, and in 1950 painted murals for Harkness Graduate Center Dining Room at Harvard University. Miró's work had a great influence on other artists in the USA.

During World War II, Miró had worked with the Spanish potter Llorens Artigas, and from 1954 to 1959 he devoted himself exclusively to pottery. In 1955, he was commissioned to create large-scale works for the UNESCO Building in Paris and for these he developed a completely new style of ceramic (made of clay) wall design.

In 1956, Miró moved to Palma in Mallorca, which was to remain his home until the end of his life. He continued to create murals, pavements and sculptures and died on 25 December 1983 at the age of 90.

Harlequin's Carnival, by Joan Miró (1924–25)
This work looks like a party of energetic forms cavorting in a room. The musical stave on the wall suggests that the room is full of lively sound, which the shapes are dancing to. They bounce on coils, jump from ladders and swim through the air, in contrast to the calm of the night scene glimpsed through the window.

Man Ray 1890–1976

- Born 27 August 1890 in Philadelphia, USA.
- Died 18 November 1976 in Paris.

Key works
The Gift, 1921
Glass Tears, 1930
Observatory Time, 1932–34

Man Ray's parents were Russian Jews who had emigrated to the USA. He was named Emanuel Radnitsky and was teased at school because of his foreign name. When he was seven his family moved to Brooklyn, New York.

The young Emanuel was interested in art from an early age, and at school he took classes in art and technical drawing. In 1908, he turned down a grant to study architecture saying that he was only interested in the interiors of buildings. He attended life drawing and watercolour classes at the Ferrer Center in New York City and began to visit the **avant-garde** '291' Gallery of the experimental photographer Alfred Stieglitz. In 1912, he moved to Ridgefield, New Jersey, where he worked as a draughtsman in an advertising company. In his early twenties he decided to shorten his name to Man Ray.

In 1913, Man Ray visited the Armory Show in New York and saw the work of daring European artists such as Marcel Duchamp and Francis Picabia. He began to work in a **Cubist** style. In 1914, he had his first one-man show, and was introduced to Marcel Duchamp who became a lifelong friend. He moved to New York where he helped to start the New York **Dada** movement, experimenting with new techniques in painting and photography. Man Ray said of his experiments with photography, 'I am trying to make my photography automatic – to use my camera as I would a typewriter'.

In 1918, Man Ray experimented with a spray gun to make his 'aerograph' series of paintings which closely resembled photographs, and in 1920 he exhibited a sewing machine wrapped in a blanket, calling it *Enigma of Isadore Ducasse*. When Duchamp returned to Paris he invited Man Ray to go with him. Man Ray jumped at the chance. He packed his equipment into a trunk, but forgot to pack any clothes, spent his last night in New York partying and was delivered by his friends onto the boat an hour before departure. He arrived in Paris in July 1921 where he was warmly welcomed by the Dadaists, and given a one-man show. In 1922, he published a collection of photos called *Delicious Fields*, and took part in the first international Dada exhibition.

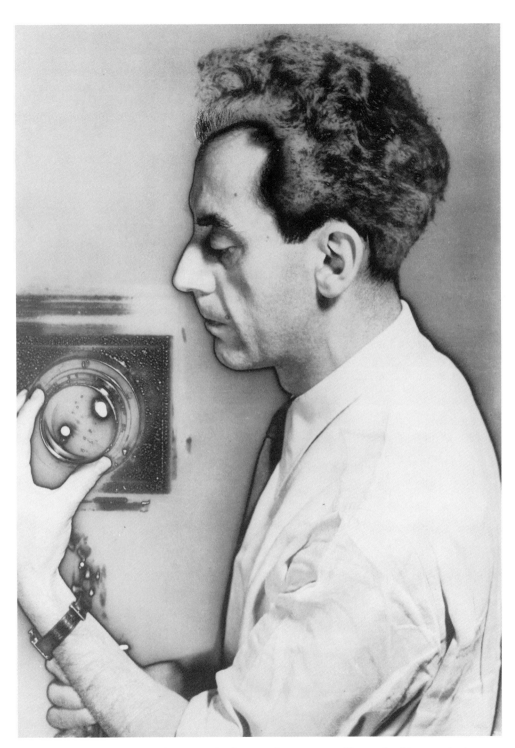

▓▓▓ *Here we see Man Ray focusing the lens on his camera. He worked innovatively with photography inventing new words for new developing processes, and using his own name in the term Rayograph to describe abstract pictures made by placing objects on light-sensitive photographic paper.*

Man Ray became part of the Surrealist movement in Paris, and from 1923 his main interest was making films including *Anemic Cinema*, *Emak Bakia* and *Star of the Sea*. In 1921, he developed a type of photograph where the ghost of the photographed object appeared on the paper. He called these photographs 'rayograms', in a deliberate pun on his name. Man Ray made rayograms of things he found around him such as drawing pins and salt.

'This is the principle of the rayogram ... Various objects, whatever one wishes, are placed in the dark on a sheet of light-sensitive paper. This combination is then illuminated by a ray of light ... When the paper exposed in this way is developed, the rayogram appears as white silhouettes and incredibly delicately graduated shadows. The effect is absolutely unique to this kind of technique.'

By 1923, Man Ray was becoming successful as a photographer. One of his most famous photographs of this time was the blurred photographic image of Marquesa Casati with three sets of eyes, which she described as 'the portrait of

■■■ *La Fortune*, by Man Ray (1938)
Painted a year before the outbreak of World War II, this work, mysteriously entitled Fortune *or* Luck *shows a billiard table in a desert below a sky of solid and improbable looking clouds.*

her soul'. In 1925, he made a series of nudes of Kiki of Montparnasse, with whom he lived for six years, and a set of studies of the Surrealist artist Meret Oppenheim shown against the wheel of an **etching** press with her hand covered in black ink. In the same year his fashion photographs were published in both the French and the American editions of *Vogue* magazine.

In 1929, Man Ray took on a new photographic assistant, a 22-year-old former model, called Lee Miller. She was his assistant, model and lover until 1932.

In the summer of 1940, Man Ray left Paris for the USA and made his way to Hollywood where he met the 29-year-old Juliet Browner. During the 1940s he participated in many exhibitions and held several one-man shows. In 1946 he married Juliet Browner in Beverly Hills in a double wedding with Max Ernst and Dorothea Tanning.

In 1951, Man Ray moved back to Paris with Juliet and after this she was the only model he ever used. In Paris he experimented with colour photography and began painting again. He continued to work with great success. He died in Paris aged 86.

Lee Miller 1907–77

The American photographer Lee Miller studied art briefly in Paris before returning to the USA to study painting, theatre design and lighting in New York. For a short while she worked for *Vogue* magazine as a writer, photographer and model, but from 1929 to 1932 she lived with Man Ray in Paris and worked with him as his photographic assistant. Miller was not only the creator of memorable photographs, but also the model for many Surrealist photographs. She described herself as looking like an angel with a devil inside. After separating from Man Ray, she worked as a freelance photographer in the Middle East, and as a war correspondent. In 1947 she married Roland Penrose, and moved to England.

Yves Tanguy 1900–55

- Born 5 January 1900 in Paris, France
- Died 15 January 1955 in Woodbury, Connecticut, USA.

Key works
Mama, Papa is wounded!, 1927
Days of Delay, 1937
Through Birds, Through Line but not Through Glass, 1943

Yves Tanguy's father was a ship's captain from Brittany, in northern France and family holidays were spent in Brittany, where the rocky landscape made a lasting impression on the young artist. In 1918, Tanguy joined the merchant navy as a cabin boy, and spent two years sailing to Africa and South America.

In 1922, after two years of **military service**, Tanguy settled in Paris, working at a number of unusual jobs. He worked in an agency that provided clippings from newspapers, as a tram driver, and as a maker of toasted sandwiches. He was a self-taught artist whose inspiration to paint sprung from a sighting of *The Child's Brain* by Giorgio de Chirico. He caught sight of this painting from the platform of a bus and jumped from the moving bus to examine it more closely. The painting fired his imagination and was the springboard for his art.

■ *Photographed by Man Ray, Tanguy is shown looking directly into the camera with a wide-eyed and fixed stare. The suggestion of energy is reflected not only in his eyes and pose but in his distinctive electric shock effect hairstyle.*

During 1924, Tanguy painted humorous pictures, read early issues of *La Révolution Surréaliste* and began to take a great interest in Surrealism. In 1925, he met André Breton, who became a close friend. Tanguy became a Surrealist painter, creating works which do not show objects or scenes that we can recognize. Tanguy's paintings show jelly-like shapes moving on surfaces, which look as though they could be the sea bed or the surface of the moon. Breton described Tanguy as a 'painter of subterranean and oceanic marvels'.

Tanguy produced a space–age vision several decades before the first moon landing. The strange forms in many of his paintings probably reflect his fascination with curious rock formations.

Tanguy's paintings were not planned in advance. Instead he always insisted on using **automatism** and painted whatever came into his head: 'I found that if I planned a picture beforehand, it never surprised me, and surprises are my pleasure in painting.' Tanguy let his **unconscious** mind produce pictures which the viewer is left to puzzle over, producing the effect of waking from a disturbing and perplexing dream. By 1939, André Breton saw Tanguy as Salvador Dalí's most important rival. Breton believed that the Surrealists, led by Tanguy, were returning to automatism as their main method of creating pictures.

In 1939, Tanguy met the American Surrealist painter Kay Sage in Paris, and they married a year later. War had broken out in Europe, and Tanguy decided to emigrate, setting sail for America with Sage. Tanguy toured the USA and travelled in Canada, before settling in Woodbury, Connecticut. He died from a blood clot on the brain when he was only 55.

Through Birds, Through Line but not Through Glass, by Yves Tanguy (1943)
The title is deliberately confusing but shows Tanguy's use of biomorphic forms (irregular abstract forms based on shapes found in nature). Here we read the image as spacecraft that has landed on the seabed.

Dorothea Tanning b. 1910

- Born 25 August 1910 in Galesburg, Illinois, USA.
- Has lived in Sweden, USA and France.

Key works
Birthday, 1942
Eine Kleine Nachtmusik, 1943
The Mirror, 1950

▮▮ *Photographed by Lee Miller, Man Ray's photographic assistant, Tanning is shown with her husband in 1946, the year they were married.*

Dorothea Tanning was the second of three sisters. Her mother was American and her father was Swedish. The girls had a strict religious upbringing, but this did not prevent them from being dressed in the finest clothes of velvet and lace. At seven, Tanning was a natural Surrealist. She created cubes of paper which she covered in messages to her secret loves. She listened to the sound of the noise of the paper and dreamt of the words they contained.

Tanning began to study art but abandoned the course after only two weeks, because she felt sure that painting could not be taught. So she worked in a restaurant, and for a puppet theatre before travelling to New York where she posed for photographers and painters. Tanning did not believe in the importance of people's pasts and created an alternative history for herself. She said that from an early age she had believed that she was a stag in a forest.

By 1935, Tanning was working in New York as a freelance commercial artist, and the following year she saw an exhibition of **Dadaist** and Surrealist artists in New York. This proved a huge revelation to her, and she decided to travel to Paris, heart of the Surrealist world, where she arrived in 1939 at the outbreak of war. She stayed only briefly as it seemed safer to move to Stockholm in Sweden. There she stayed with her uncle Hugo and other family members who she used as models for her paintings.

Tanning returned to the USA in 1940. She made designs for Macy's department store, and the following year she had an exhibition of her fabrics. In 1941, she married Homer Shannon, but separated from him six months later.

Many of the Surrealists were in exile in the USA during World War II, and Tanning found herself among like-minded artists. In 1942, she met her dream companion – the German-born artist Max Ernst, who later abandoned his wife, Peggy Guggenheim, for her. Tanning and Ernst moved to Sedona, Arizona. In 1944 she had her first solo exhibition in New York, and the following year began work designing the sets for George Balanchine's ballet *The Night Shadow*, which were greatly praised.

In 1946 Tanning married Ernst in Beverly Hills in a double wedding with Man Ray and Juliet Browner. Many Surrealists came to visit Ernst and Tanning in Arizona – including Man Ray, Duchamp, Tanguy, Lee Miller and Roland Penrose. In 1949, Balanchine **commissioned** Tanning to work on designs for another ballet, *The Witch*. Her success led to more commissions for the ballets *Bayou* and *Will o' the Wisp*.

Tanning travelled in Italy during 1954, and bought a farmhouse in France. When Ernst failed to get US citizenship, he and Tanning returned to France where they lived and worked in Paris and in their farmhouse in the country.

In 1976, Ernst died, and Tanning was beside herself with grief, suffering from a mental collapse the following year. Eventually, she returned to work and exhibited almost annually from 1986 to 1993 in the Camden Arts Centre in London. Tanning now lives in New York and continues to write poetry, paint and draw.

Eine Kleine Nachtmusik (A Little Night Music), by Dorothea Tanning (1943)
This title is taken from a work of music by Mozart, and in no way helps us to interpret the strange and sinister painting in which two girls on a hotel landing seem to be menaced by a giant sunflower. The hair of one girl is standing on end as though shot through with an electric shock. The hair on the other figure does not stick to the head, making us see her not as a girl, but as a doll.

The Next Generation

Surrealism is one of the most important art movements of the 20th century. It was about the transformation of life, the random and the absurd, and the power of the dream and the subconscious. It was practised across all the art forms: painting, sculpture, poetry, film, jewellery, dress and ceramic design.

Principally an inter-war phenomenon based in Paris, the influence of Surrealism spread beyond France to other European cities and the USA. The impact of Surrealist art was particularly felt in New York where many of the principal Surrealists lived during World War II. This group of artists, including Dalí, Ernst, Masson, Man Ray and Tanning, had a powerful impact on the

Quarantania I, by Louise Bourgeois (1947–53)
The sculpture represents five tall bodies. All of the bodies are attached to a wooden base, which prompted Bourgeois to suggest: 'They are dependent on each other for better or worse.'

young American artists of the next generation. Their ideas about the **unconscious** forming the subject of art was very important. Duchamp was also a big influence in modern art. He broke down the barrier between art and life and was the creator of 'conceptual art' in which the idea behind the work of art was the most important concept – not how well the work of art was made or painted.

Long after the Surrealist movement had ceased to exist, its influence has continued to be felt across the spectrum of the arts – not just in painting and sculpture, but in advertising and film.

Louise Bourgeois b. 1911

After settling in New York in 1938 the Paris-born Bourgeois spent World War II working with Joan Miró and André Masson, who later influenced her work in the same way they had influenced Pollock – by tapping into the unconscious. Her use of non-traditional materials, such as wire mesh, mirrors, bottles and light also reflects the influence of the Surrealists.

Jackson Pollock 1912–56

The Abstract Expressionist artist Jackson Pollock wrote that he was 'particularly impressed with the concept of the source of art being the unconscious'. He was a great admirer of Miró and the way he seemed to be able to tap into the unconscious part of his mind to produce images from within. The influence of Ernst is also evident in Pollock's painting *Untitled (Naked Man)* with its bird head/minotaur figure, reminiscent of Ernst's work.

Andy Warhol 1928–87

The American Pop Artist Andy Warhol responded to the strangeness of Surrealist art, especially to the work of Magritte whom he described as a really great artist. He also saw a parallel in the work he was doing with that of Dalí, saying: 'When Salvador Dalí used to come round to the Factory in the 1960s, he thought he had done everything we were doing. We thought it was new, but we were doing things he had already done.'

Timeline

1887 Jean Arp born 16 September; Marcel Duchamp born 28 July

1890 Man Ray born 27 August

1891 Max Ernst born 2 April

1893 Joan Miró born 20 April

1896 André Masson born 4 January

1897 Paul Delvaux born 23 September

1898 René Magritte born 21 November

1900 Yves Tanguy born 5 January; Freud publishes *The Interpretation of Dreams*

1901 Alberto Giacometti born 10 October

1904 Salvador Dalí born 11 May

1907 Frida Kahlo born 6 July

1910 Dorothea Tanning born 25 August

1914 World War I begins

1916 **Dada** is founded

1918 World War I ends

1919 Breton experiments with **automatic** writing

1920 Last major Dada exhibition, in Cologne

1921 Breton visits Freud in Vienna

1924 Breton publishes his first *Surrealist Manifesto;* first issue of *La Révolution Surréaliste*

1925 First Surrealist exhibition in Paris

1926 Man Ray produces the film *Emak Bakia;* Belgian Surrealist group is founded

1928 Breton publishes *Surrealism and Painting;* Dalí and Buñuel produce the film *Un Chien Andalou*

1930 Breton publishes his second *Surrealist Manifesto;* first issue of *Surrealism in the Service of the Revolution*

1933 First issue of *Minotaur*

1936 First exhibition of Surrealist objects in Paris; International Surrealist exhibition in London; Spanish Civil War begins

1938 International Surrealist exhibitions in Paris and Amsterdam

1939 World War II begins; many Surrealists move to New York

1942 Breton gives lecture to students at Yale on 'The Situation of Surrealism' between the two world wars

1947 Breton and Duchamp organize the International Surrealist Exhibition at the Galerie Maeght, Paris; Breton founds 'Cause', to co-ordinate different national Surrealist groups

Glossary

abstract non-representational, not depicting an object, landscape or person of identifiable form

atheist a person who does not believe in God

automatic painting or writing without using the thinking part of the brain in order to get in touch with inner emotion

automatism the process of writing without using the thinking part of the brain

avant-garde new, cutting edge, disturbing art; pioneers or innovators in any area of the arts

collage a piece of art made up of a variety of different materials – cuttings from newspapers, string, fabric and paint, for example

commission something an artist is asked to create by someone else

cosmic universal, immense

Cubism modern art movement founded by Picasso and Braque in 1907 in which all elements of the painting are fragmented and the colour is subdued

Dada forerunner of the Surrealist movement, which flourished between 1916 and 1922. Dada art did not have to make sense and tried to break down barriers between art forms.

deface destroy the external appearance of something

der Blaue Reiter Blue Rider group; German Expressionist art movement formed in 1911

etching printing process involving the copying of an image on to a metal plate, which is then covered in ink and pressed over paper to produce a copy of the original

fanatic zealot, excessively enthusiastic

found object something found rather than made by the artist

free association allowing the mind to wander from one thought to another

futility uselessness

innovative radically new

manifesto public statement of the policy or aims of a particular group or society

military service compulsory military service in the armed forces demanded of all male school leavers

motif dominant idea or feature of a composition

mural picture painted directly on to the wall

occult secret, hidden, concerned with dark forces and devil worship

October Revolution a revolutionary uprising against the Russian aristocracy in 1917 led by Lenin

Post-Impressionist term that covers several variations on Impressionist painting; colourful, freely painted works of everyday subject matter

radical new, revolutionary

ready-made an object found, not made by the artist, like a bicycle wheel

relief a non-two dimensional work of art with slightly raised elements

representational easily recognized as being an object, person or landscape

Section d'Or an exhibition held in 1912 by a group of Cubists who linked Cubism to the technological advances currently happening

Symbolism art movement focusing on dreams and literature, which flourished between 1880 and 1900

unconscious the non-thinking part of the brain

Resources

List of famous works
Jean Arp (1887–1966)
Birds in an Aquarium, c.1920, Museum of Modern Art, New York
Overturned Blue Shoe With Two Heels Under a Black Vault, c. 1925,
Guggenheim Museum, New York
Head: Scottish Lips, 1927, Geraldine Galateau
Garland of Buds, 1936, Guggenheim Museum, New York

Salvador Dali (1904–89)
The Persistence of Memory, 1931, Museum of Modern Art, New York
Autumn Cannibalism, 1936, Tate Modern, London
Metamorphosis of Narcissus, 1937, Tate Modern, London
Lobster Telephone, 1937, Tate Modern, London
Christ of St John of the Cross, 1951, Glasgow Gallery of Art

Paul Delvaux (1897–1994)
Dawn over the City, 1940, Artesia Bank, Belgium
Sleeping Venus, 1944, Tate Modern, London
A Mermaid in Full Moonlight, 1949, Southampton Gallery of Art

Marcel Duchamp (1887–1968)
The Large Glass, 1915–23, Tate Modern, London
Fountain, 1917, Museum of Modern Art, New York
L.H.O.O.Q., 1919, Tate Modern, London

Max Ernst (1891–1976)
Of This Men Shall Know Nothing, 1923, Tate Modern, London
Pietà or Revolution by Night, 1923, Tate Modern, London
The Forest, 1927-28, Guggenheim Museum, New York

Alberto Giacometti (1901–66)
Suspended Ball, 1930-31
Three Figures Outdoors, 1929, Art Gallery of Ontario, Toronto
The Cage, 1930–31, Moderna Museet, Stockholm
Woman with her Throat Cut, 1932, Scottish National Gallery, Edinburgh

Frida Kahlo (1907–54)
Self-portrait Dedicated to Leon Trotsky, 1937, National Museum of Women in
the Arts, Washington DC
Self-portrait with Monkey, 1940, Private collection
Self-portrait with Hair Cut Off, 1940, Museum of Modern Art, New York

René Magritte (1898–1967)
The Assassin Threatened, 1926, Museum of Modern Art, New York
The Lovers, 1928, Museum of Modern Art, New York
Red Model, 1935, Moderna Museet, Stockholm
Time Transfixed, 1938, Art Institute of Chicago

André Masson (1896–1987)
Battle of Fishes, 1926, Museum of Modern Art, New York
Children of the Island, 1926–27, Private Collection
Ariadne's Thread, 1938, Private Collection
Gradiva, 1939, Private Collection

Joan Miró (1893–1983)
The Kerosene Lamp, 1924, Art Institute of Chicago
The Harlequin's Carnival, 1924-25, Albright Knox Gallery, Buffalo
The Policeman, 1925, Art Institute of Chicago
Person Throwing a Stone at a Bird, 1926, Museum of Modern Art, New York
Dog Barking at the Moon, 1926, Philadelphia Museum Of Art
Landscape (The Hare), 1927, Guggenheim Museum, New York

Man Ray (1890–1976)
Self-portrait, 1916, Getty Museum, Los Angeles
The Gift, 1921, Museum of Modern Art, New York
Return to Reason, 1921, Minneapolis Institute of Arts
Peggy Guggenheim, 1924, Rijksmuseum, Amsterdam
Observatory Time, 1932–34, Private collection

Yves Tanguy (1900–55)
Mama, Papa is wounded!, 1927, Museum of Modern Art, New York
Days of Delay, 1937, Musée d'Art Moderne, Paris
Moonscape, Tate Modern, London

Dorothea Tanning (b. 1910)
Birthday, 1942, Philadelphia Museum of Art
Eine Kleine Nachtmusik, 1943, Tate Modern, London
The Mirror, 1950, Arno Schfler

Where to see Surrealist art

UK
Tate Gallery, London
Brighton Art Museum
Dalí Universe, County Hall, London

USA
Salvador Dalí Museum, St Petersburg, Florida
Museum of Modern Art, New York
Metropolitan Museum of Art, New York

Europe
Dalí museum, Figueras, Spain
Fundacio Joan Miró, Palma, Mallorca
Musée Royaux des Beaux-Arts, Brussels, Belgium
Paul Delvaux Museum, Saint Idesbalt, Belgium

Useful websites

www.surrealist.com/new
www.salvadordalimuseum.org
www.magritte.com
www.manray–photo.com

Internet Disclaimer
All the Internet addresses (URLs) given in this book were valid at the time of going to press.
However, due to the dynamic nature of the Internet, some addresses may have changed, or sites
may have ceased to exist since publication. While the author and publishers regret any
inconvenience this may cause readers, no responsibility for any such changes can be accepted by
either the author or the publishers.

Further Reading

Most of the biographies listed are written for adults, but feature many reproductions of the artist's work, which will be interesting to young readers.

General

Surrealism in the series: Art Revolutions, Linda Bolton, Belitha Press, 2000

Surrealism in the series: Movements in Modern Art, Fiona Bradley, Tate Gallery, 2000

The artists

Arp: Reliefs, Jean Arp, Henry Moore Sculpture Trust, 1995

Dali's Mustache, by Salvador Dalí and Philippe Halsman, Flammarian, 1994

Salvador Dali, Mike Venezia, from the Getting to Know the World's Greatest Artists and Composers, Watts, 1994

The Essential Salvador Dali, Robert Glogg, HH Abrams, 1998

Max Ernst: Retrospective, Werner Spies (Introduction), Tate Gallery, Prestel Publishing Ltd, 1991

Giacometti, James Lord, Phoenix Press, 1996

The Diary of Frida Kahlo, Frida Kahlo and Carlos Fuentes (Introduction), Bloomsbury, 1998

Adventures in Art: Now You See It – Now You Don't: Magritte by Angela Wenzel, Prestel, 1998

Magritte, A M Hammacher, Thames and Hudson, 1986

Miró in his Studio, Juan Punyet Miro, Thames and Hudson, 1996

Man Ray, Jed Perl, Aperture, 1997

Man Ray's Celebrity Portrait Photographs, Dover Publications, 1995

Between Lives: An Artist and her World, Dorothea Tanning, W. W. Norton, 2001

Index

Titles in the *Artists in Profile* series include:

Hardback   0 431 11650 4

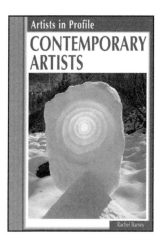

Hardback   0 431 11653 9

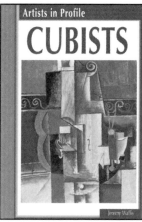

Hardback   0 431 11642 3

Hardback   0 431 11643 1

Hardback   0 431 11640 7

Hardback   0 431 11651 2

Hardback   0 431 11641 5

Hardback   0 431 11652 0

Find out about the other titles in this series on our website www.heinemann.co.uk/library